Electric Pressure Cooker Cookbook: 100 Electric Pressure Cooker Recipes

Delicious, Quick and Easy To Prepare Pressure Cooker Recipes with an Easy Step By Step Guide to Electric Pressure Cooking

By **Jenny Jameson**

Table of Contents

Introduction

The electric pressure cooker is a great tool that you are going to fall in love with. It allows you the opportunity to cook time consuming meals in a matter of minutes. You can get a big roast done in 10 minutes, pork chops in 8, and desserts in even less time.

This cookbook is going to show you just how great the pressure cooker is. It starts out with a short introduction about the pressure cooker and tips to help you to get started. The majority is comprised of 100 recipes that you will love. There are options for chicken, beef, soups, desserts, pork, vegetarian, and so much more.

The next time that you need to make a great meal for your family but you are limited on time, check out this cookbook and get started right now!

Reviews Request

Please help out a busy Mom and beginner author by leaving a review. It only takes a few minutes and means the world to me.

An Introduction to Pressure Cooking

Electric pressure cooking is a great way to make a meal in no time at all. Many great meals that would normally take you all day to get done can be done in less than twenty minutes with the help of a pressure cooker.

And there are no limits to the foods that you can cook whether they are a variety of meats, vegetables, potatoes, and rice.

You will even be able to make soups and desserts. This chapter will discuss some of the ways to make pressure cooking easier.

Temperature and Pressure Ratios

You will be able to cook your food much more quickly than what was possible using the oven, stove, or slow cooker when you choose a pressure cooker.

While using the pressure cooker, you will be able to get the food cooked at lower temperatures. The translation for the different pressures and temperatures that correspond with them are:

Low Pressure—this will translate into 220 degrees for cooking and 3 psi.

Medium Pressure—this will translate into 235 degrees for cooking and 10 psi.

High Pressure—this will translate into 250 degrees for cooking and 13-15 psi.

Tips for Poultry and Meat

The electric pressure cooker is a great way to cook up the poultry and meat that you need for your meals. Often you will decide not to make a meal because the meat is going to take all day to cook and you just do not have time or did not think about it in time to prepare it.

The pressure cooker is meant to help you to make these meals anyway because you are only going to need less than ten minutes to heat up the whole meal.

If you decide to make a delicious meal with your pressure cooker, here are some tips that you can follow for cooking poultry and meat: Pat the meat dry before you season with salt or other seasonings that you are using.

Sear and then brown the meat in oil before doing the rest of the recipe in order to get the best texture and flavor unless it is specifically stated in the recipe to not do this. You can choose to use poultry either without or with the skin

Tougher meats that are less expensive are going to do better in the pressure cooker. This is because using the pressure cooking method is going to break down the fibers in the meat in order to end up with fork tender results even in tough meats.

Always let the whole poultry and cooked roasts sit for about 15 minutes after cooking before taking the time to carve them. When slicing your roast, slice it against the grain.

These are just a few of the tips that are going to help you to cook your meats in the way that you would like to make fantastic meals every time.

Tips for Pressure Cooking Success

While pressure cookers are able to save you a lot of time while making great meals for your whole family, this process can sometimes be confusing when you are getting started. Here are some tips to help you get started:

Brown your meat and some vegetables—this is going to help them to get more of a crisp flavor each time. Make sure to do this with some oil and do it in small batches even if you are cooking a lot of food. When you are done, deglaze the pot to get more of the flavor before finishing the rest of the meal.

Limit the liquid—many people feel like they will need to add in more liquid to their meals to prevent it from getting dry. This is not something to worry about with the pressure cooker because the food is cooked in a sealed pot so there is not the issue with evaporation. Usually about a cup of liquid is going to be enough to cook the meal.

Do not overfill the pressure cooker—it should never be filled to over 2/3 full of the food you are cooking. Also, try not to pack the food too much inside the cooker. If you do not follow these things the cooker is not going to be able to operate the right way.

Even pieces cook better—food needs to be as close to uniform in size as possible so that it all cooks the same.

Stop and go cooking—if some of the ingredients are going to cook with a variety of times, you should start with the foods that are slow to cook first. When those are done, stop the cooking and add in the faster ones. This is going to allow you to cook all of the ingredients so they are done about the same time.

Start high, end low—when cooking, you will need to start with a high heat. When the pressure you want is reached, lower in order to simmer for best results.

Set timers—it is hard to keep track of time when you are busy cooking and since the pressure cooker goes so quickly, you will really need to keep track of it. Turn on a timer to help you keep track and get the food done just right.

Releasing pressure—when your food is done, you should use the right release method for the pressure to make sure that it is safe and the food is prepared correctly.

The pressure cooker is the perfect way to make some amazing meals without having to spend all day on it. With the right tips and the best recipes, you will always have the perfect meal to satisfy the whole family.

Buffalo Chicken Wings

Ingredients:

2 lbs. chicken wings
1 lb. trimmed celery
Coating
¼ c. honey
4 Tbsp. hot sauce
¼ c. tomato puree
3 tsp. salt
Sauce
1 Tbsp. parsley
1 c. plain yogurt

Directions:

1. Turn on the pressure cooker and place a cup of water inside as well as the steamer basket.
2. If the wings are still in whole pieces, separate out each and slice through the skin all the way to the joint.
3. Place all of the wings into the steamer basket. Close and then lock the lid of your cooker and turn the heat up so that it is on higher. When the pressure is reached you can turn it down a little, but maintain the pressure. Cook like this for 10 minutes.
4. While the wings are cooking, take out a bowl and combine the salt, tomato puree, honey, and hot sauce. Mix well so that everything is combined.
5. When the wings are done, open up the cook so that the pressure is released. Take the wings out and then tumble them around in the sauce to coat them evenly.

6. Place the wings onto some paper and slide so they are in the broiler for around 5 minutes to become crispy and brown.
7. While the chicken is in the broiler you can place the yogurt and celery sticks on a serving platter.
8. When the chicken is done, brush with any of the sauce before placing onto the platter.

Chicken Liver Pate

Ingredients:

¾ lb. chicken livers
1 bay leaf
1 chopped onion
¼ c. red wine
1 Tbsp. capers
2 anchovies
Salt
Pepper
1 Tbsp. butter

Directions:

1. Place a bit of olive oil into the pressure cooker. Place the salt, pepper, and onion into the pressure cooker and turn on to medium heat in order to soften up the onion.
2. Add in the bay leaf and chicken livers, swirling everything about for two minutes so that the livers can become seared.
3. Add the red wine and then use a spoon to rub down the brown bits that get stuck inside the pan. At this time you can close and then lock the lid of your cooker and turn up the heat to a high setting. When the cooker reaches the right pressure, lower the heat a bit and then cook for 5 minutes.
4. When this time is over, open up the cooker to release pressure. Remove and get rid of the bay leaf and then add the capers and anchovies
5. Puree the cooker contents and then taste to see if it tastes good. Fold in the butter which can melt with the heat and then mix it well.
6. Transfer to a container to serve with herbs to garnish. Chill a bit before serving with some bread slices

Prosciutto Rolls and Chicken

Ingredients:

6 prosciutto slices
6 chicken breasts
10 sage leaves
1 Tbsp. olive oil
1 Tbsp. butter
¼ c. dry white wine
1 tsp. salt
¾ c. chicken stock
1 c. peas

Directions:

1. Cover your meat with some wax paper and then use a mallet to pound it into even thickness. Lay out the breast so the square side is pointing up. Cover with the slices of prosciutto well and then fasten so it is closed with a skewer or a toothpick.
2. When the cooker is heated up, melt the butter inside before adding in the sage leaves and the oil. Raise the heat to a high setting and let the chicken rolls brown. When this happens on all sides, pour the wine all around the chicken. Allow the wine to become almost all the way evaporated before adding the peas, salt, and stock on top.
3. Close the pressure cooker and then turn the heat so it is at high. When it reaches the right pressure, lower a bit. Cook this for 5 minutes at the high pressure.
4. When this is done, open up the cooker to release the pressure. Serve this with the peas and the liquid. You can also add in some polenta and mashed potatoes and enjoy.

Whole Chicken

Ingredients:

3 lb. chicken
1 can of beer
Braise
½ can of beer
2 bay leaves
1 squeezed lemon
Seasoning
2 Tbsp. chopped rosemary
2 Tbsp. chopped thyme
2 Tbsp. chopped sage
2 Tbsp. olive oil
Juice from a lemon
Pepper
½ tsp. salt

Directions:

1. Rinse and then dry the chicken all over and then pat dry. Then you can work on the seasoning. Bring out a bowl and mix the pepper, salt, lemon, olive oil, and herbs. Tuck the wings behind the neck of the chicken and then brush these seasonings on.
2. Take out a pan and brown the chicken on all sides, which is going to take 10 minutes. While that is happening you can prepare the slow cooker. Pour the beer into the can and place half of the lemon zest and one of the bay leaves inside the beer can. Take the other leaf and the rest of the zest into the pan and then put the can in the middle of the pan.
3. Now you can lower the chicken inside the pressure cooker, sitting it over the beer can. Before you close the cooker, pour any of the leftover seasoning on top of the chicken.

4. Close and then lock the pressure cooker and turn it to a high heat. When it gets there, lower the heat a bit and then let the chicken cook for 20 minutes.
5. When cooking is done, open the pressure cooker and then slowly take the chicken out. Place onto a serving platter and tent with foil.
6. Turn the heat up in the cooker and let this cook for 5 minutes without the lid. Strain it out and pour on top of the chicken. Sprinkle on some fresh herbs and then serve.

Lemon Braised Chicken

Ingredients:

3 juiced lemons
3 rosemary sprigs
2 garlic cloves
2 sprigs sage
4 Tbsp. olive oil
Pepper
½ parsley leave bunch
Extra Ingredients
½ c. dry white wine
1 chicken
4 oz. olives
1 lemon

Directions:

1. Work on the marinade by chopping together the parsley, sage, rosemary, and garlic. Put them in a container before adding the pepper, salt, olive oil, and lemon juice.
2. Take the chicken and remove the skin. Place into a deep dish before covering with the marinade. Cover and let marinate for a few hours.
3. Turn on the pressure cooker and leave the lid off. Add in some oil and then brown your chicken on each side for 5 minutes. De glaze your cooker with the white wine for 3 minutes so that the wine is almost gone without the chicken inside.
4. Place the chicken in and the pour the rest of the marinade over it. You can add some water into the cooker if you need later on.
5. Close the lid of the cooker and turn it up to a high heat. When it reaches the pressure, lower a bit and then cook the chicken for 10 minutes.

6. When this is done, open the cooker to release the pressure. Take the chicken out of your cooker and place onto a platter covered up with foil.
7. Let the liquid in the cooker reduce without the lid on until it is syrupy and thick. Lower the heat before placing the chicken back in to warm up. Mix it with the glaze and let it simmer for another 5 minutes.
8. Sprinkle the chicken with lemon slices, olives, and rosemary. Serve right away.

Chicken Broth

Ingredients:

6 c. water
2 celery pieces
1 carrot
1 sliced onion
1 Tbsp. parsley
1 garlic clove
¼ tsp. sage
1 pkg. chicken giblets
Salt
Pepper

Directions

1. To start, cut the garlic cloves, onion, celery, and carrot into big pieces.
2. Take out the pressure cooker and place the basket inside. Place your vegetables inside before adding in the giblets, spices, and water.
3. Turn the cooker on to a high setting and let the ingredients cook for 15 minutes. After it is done, release the pressure and lift the basket out.
4. Pour some broth into prepared glass jars, place into the fridge overnight, and then skim the fat from the top before using.

Chicken Adobo

Ingredients:

1 cut up chicken
½ c. soy sauce
¼ c. vinegar
1 garlic clove
1 onion
3 bay leaves
1 piece ginger
Water for half of water

Directions:

1. Cut up the chicken into small pieces so that it is able to fit into the pressure cooker easier.
2. Turn on the cooker and place the chicken inside with the rest of the ingredients. Place the lid on top and turn on high to get pressure going before turning down the heat a bit.
3. Cook the chicken for 45 minutes. When it is done, take the chicken out and keep warm. Keep up the heat without the lid on for about 5 minutes in order to thicken the gravy.
4. Pour the gravy on top of the chicken and then serve the whole meal over some rice before enjoying.

Moroccan Chicken

Ingredients:

1 butternut squash
1 Tbsp. olive oil
3 carrots
3 sliced onions
3 lb. cut up chicken
3 minced garlic cloves
2 tsp. cumin
1 Tbsp. ginger, grated
2 tsp. coriander
16 oz. can chickpeas
Cayenne pepper
Salt
½ c. raisins

Directions:

1. Peel and cut up the squash into small chunks. Take the carrots and cut into half inch pieces.
2. Bring out the pressure cooker and heat up the olive oil inside. Place the chicken inside as well and let it brown on all sides before removing.
3. Place the onions inside and let them cook for 10 minutes so that they become golden. Add in some cayenne pepper, salt, spices, ginger, and garlic and cook for a minute before adding the chicken back in with the squash and ¼ a cup of water.
4. Place the lid on the cooker and bring the pressure up. Let the heat go down a bit and then cook it all for 15 minutes.
5. When this is done, release the pressure before adding in the carrots, raisins, and chickpeas. Return the pressure up before lowering the heat again and cooking for another 5 minutes. Serve warm.

Italian Chicken

Ingredients:
4 Italian sausage links
1 Tbsp. olive oil
1 chicken with skin off and cut up
1 onion
2 garlic cloves
2 green bell peppers
¾ tsp. basil
1 can tomatoes, diced
Red pepper flakes
¼ tsp. fennel seeds
Salt & Pepper

Directions:

1. Heat the oil up in the pressure cooker. While that is heating up, prick the sausages in a few places using a fork.
2. When the oil is warmed up add the chicken and the sausage into the pressure cooker and then cook them until they are browned on all sides.
3. While the chicken is being cooked, dice the onion, cut the peppers into strips, and mince the garlic.
4. Once the meats are browned, take them out of the cooker and set them to the side.
5. Add the garlic, green peppers, and onion to the cooker and let them cook for around 4 minutes. Add the vinegar and then stir around the browned bits in the cooker.
6. After this time, add in the red pepper, fennel, basil, tomatoes, sausages, and chicken. Close the lid of the cooker and bring it up to a full pressure. Then you can reduce the heat and cook for about 10 minutes.
7. When the food is done, release the pressure and then add more seasonings if you need for taste. Serve warm.

Fried Chicken

Ingredients:
1 c. flour
½ tsp. flavored pepper
½ tsp. pepper
½ tsp. Adolph's tenderizer
½ tsp. poultry seasoning
¼ tsp. garlic powder
½ tsp. onion powder
½ c. milk
3 eggs
1 Tbsp. honey
Chicken cut into pieces

Directions:
1. Bring out a bowl and mix together all of the dry ingredients. Take the chicken into the dry ingredients.
2. In another bowl, mix together the honey, milk, and eggs until they are well mixed. Dip the chicken into the egg wash when it is done before coating back through the dry mix.
3. Bring out the pressure cooker. Place some hot oil inside before adding the chicken and letting it brown.
4. Place the lid on top and let the chicken cook inside the cooker for about 15 minutes. Serve the fried chicken with your favorite vegetables.

Chicken and Kraut

Ingredients:

1 jar kraut
4 chicken breasts
1 c. water
2 Tbsp. brown sugar
1 can of potatoes, whole

Directions:

1. Bring out the pressure cooker and place a bit of oil in the bottom. Turn the heat on high and then add in the chicken and let it brown a bit.
2. After the chicken is done browning you can take the chicken out before placing half of the kraut in the cooker. Add some water and half of the brown sugar and heat up for a few minutes.
3. When that is done you can add the rest of the brown sugar and kraut as well as the potatoes and chicken.
4. Place the lid back on the pressure cooker and let the ingredients cook for about 20 minutes. Release the pressure when it is done and then serve warm.

Tahitian Chicken

Ingredients:

Paprika
4 chicken breasts
2 cans orange and pineapple juice
4 Tbsp. cooking oil
½ c. butter
2 tsp. soy sauce
2 tsp. ginger

Directions:

1. Take out the chicken breasts and sprinkle on the paprika on both sides.
2. Bring out the pressure cooker and add in some oil to heat up. Once the oil is warm you can add in the chicken.
3. Using a small bowl you can combine the soy sauce, ginger, butter, and juice. Heat it up until well blended.
4. Close the lid of the pressure cooker once the ingredients are inside and then close the lid well. Turn up to a high heat and when pressure is reached, turn the heat down a bit.
5. Cook this meal for about 10 minutes before turning off the pressure cooker and releasing the pressure. Serve warm.

Chicken Jardiniere

Ingredients:
2 quartered potatoes
6 oz. chicken breasts
2 chopped carrots
2 celery stalks
2 quartered turnips
1 quartered onion
½ c. water
½ tsp. chicken broth granules

Directions:
1. Bring out the pressure cooker and spray with some cooking spray. Turn the heat on and place the chicken inside to brown on all sides.
2. When the chicken is browned you can take the chicken out. Place the rack inside and then add in the ingredients over the rack.
3. Place the cover on the pressure cooker and then bring it up to pressure by following the directions for the machine. Cook the ingredients for about 4 minutes.
4. Release the pressure and then serve the meal right away.

Oriental Chicken

Ingredients:
2 Tbsp. soy sauce
4 chicken thighs without fat or skin
1 tsp. brown sugar
¼ c. chopped onion
½ c. sliced celery
4 oz. water chestnuts
¾ c. water
1 pkg. sliced mushrooms
¼ tsp. garlic powder
1 pkg. snow peas
¼ tsp. red pepper flakes
1 tsp. cornstarch with 2 Tbsp. water

Directions:
1. Bring out a bowl and mix together all of the ingredients except the cornstarch and snow peas. Pour this into the pressure cooker.
2. Place the lid on top of the pressure cooker and then bring it up to pressure. Once it reaches pressure you can turn down the heat a bit and then let the ingredients cook for about 6 minutes.
3. When this time is up, take the lid off and add in the snow peas. Bring this mixture to a boil before adding in the cornstarch mixture. Allow everything to simmer so it can become thick.
4. Serve this over some noodles or rice and enjoy.

Viennese Chicken

Ingredients:

1 chicken cut up
1 chopped onion
1 Tbsp. oil
1 chopped bell pepper
2 carrots
1 chopped tomatoes
4 oz. drained mushrooms
½ c. water
¾ c. sour cream
Pepper
Salt
1 Tbsp. flour

Directions:

1. Take out the pressure cooker and melt the butter inside. Once the butter is melted you can brown up the pieces of chicken.
2. Take the ingredients and add them into the pressure cooker except for the flour and sour cream. Place the lid on top and let these ingredients cook under pressure for 10 minutes.
3. After this time you can take the vegetables and chicken out of the pressure cooker and put onto a serving platter.
4. Stir the sour cream and flour into the hot liquid and cook for a few minutes so that the mixture has time to thicken.
5. Pour this sauce on top of the chicken and serve with some noodles and rice.

Curried Chicken

Ingredients

1 lb. chicken cut up
2 Tbsp. peanut oil
2 Tbsp. curry powder
1 c. onion, minced
1 can of beer
1 c. apple, diced
1 tsp. salt
2 Tbsp. flour
½ tsp. pepper
1 c. yogurt

Directions:

1. Take out the pressure cooker and add in some peanut oil. Place the chicken inside and let it brown up on all sides. Add in the onions and let them sauté with the chicken for a few minutes.
2. Add the curry powder in next and stir in order to blend. Add in the pepper, salt, water, beer, and apple. Stir in order to distribute.
3. Put the lid on top of the pressure cooker and then let it heat up until the pressure is reached. Lower the heat and allow the meal to cook for about 12 minutes. When the meal is done, take it from the heat and allow too cool.
4. Allow the pressure to reduce and then open the pot and put back onto the burner. Stir around the ingredients.
5. Combine the flour and the yogurt in a bowl and add in a little bit of liquid from the pressure cooker. Pour this whole thing into the cooker and blend. Simmer for another 5 minutes on a low heat before serving with some rice.

Pineapple Chicken

Ingredients:

4 chicken breasts without skin
4 slices pineapple
3 Tbsp. soy sauce
6 oz. light beer
½ c. pineapple juice
1 Tbsp. pepper
1 onion

Directions:

1. To start, bring out the pressure cooker. Slice up the onion and place it in the bottom of the cooker before placing the chicken on top and sprinkling with the pepper.
2. Place the pineapple on top of the chicken and then cover with the mixture of beer, pineapple juice, and soy sauce. You can add more if needed.
3. Put the lid on the pressure cooker and let the chicken cook for about 20 minutes. Allow the pressure to build up and then lower the heat a bit.
4. Serve with some vegetables before enjoying

Chicken and Rice Pilaf

Ingredients:

4 chicken breasts
2 Tbsp. oil
1 chopped onion
1 c. white rice
1 can chicken broth
2 c. vegetables of choice
Cinnamon stick
1 tsp. curry
1 bay leaf

Directions:

1. Place some oil in the pressure cooker and allow it to heat up. Brown up the chicken a bit on each side so that it is golden brown all over. When it is browned you can take the chicken out and cut into small chunks.
2. Add the onions into the pot and allow them to soften for 3 minutes. After this time you can add in the rice and stir so the rice becomes coated with the onions.
3. Add the rest of your ingredients into the pressure cooker along with a little bit of water. Stir this all around. Lock the cooker into place and then turn on high. Heat so the right pressure is reached and then lower the temperature to cook. Cook for another 5 minutes before taking the lid off and taking the cinnamon and bay leaf out with a fork.
4. Place onto a plate and serve warm.

Orange and Cranberry Chicken

Ingredients:

2 Tbsp. butter
2 chicken thighs
1 chicken breast
1 chopped onion
2/3 c. cranberries
2/3 c. orange juice
1 Tbsp. honey
¼ tsp. cinnamon
¼ tsp. ginger
1/8 tsp. cloves
1/8 tsp. allspice

Directions:

1. Take out the pressure cooker and let the butter melt a bit. When this is done, place the chicken in and allow it to brown. Add the onion and cook for 5 minutes so it becomes translucent.
2. Now you can add the spices, honey, orange juice, and cranberries. Make sure to deglaze your pan and mix them all well.
3. Put the lid on the cooker and then let the pressure get high. Cook this for 8 minutes and then use a natural release method to finish cooking.
4. Serve with some cooked rice and enjoy.

Chicken and Duck Sauce

Ingredients:
3 lbs. chicken
1 Tbsp. olive oil
Salt
Pepper
¼ c. chicken broth
¼ c. white wine
½ tsp. marjoram
Sauce
¼ c. apricot preserves
1 ½ tsp. ginger root
2 Tbsp. white vinegar
2 Tbsp. honey

Directions:

1. Take out the pressure cooker and heat up the oil. When it is heated up you can add the chicken and let it brown on each side trying to be even. Take the chicken out of the cooker and then season with the marjoram, paprika, pepper, and salt
2. Drain out the fat out of the cooker and then mix the chicken broth and wine inside, taking time to scrape out any food that is stuck.
3. Now you can place the chicken back into the cooker and place the lid on top. Bring the cooker to a high pressure and cook for 8 minutes. At this time reduce the pressure and take the lid off.
4. Remove the chicken and place on the serving dish. Add in the honey, ginger, vinegar, and apricot preserves to the cooker and bring them to a boil. Cook so that the sauce can become thick, which takes around 10 minutes.
5. Spoon this sauce on the chicken and then serve.

Fricase de Pollo

Ingredients:

1 Tbsp. olive oil
½ diced red bell pepper
2 Tbsp. tomato paste
½ diced red onion
4 smashed garlic cloves
2 c. water
Salt
6 chicken leg quarters

Directions:

1. Heat the oil inside the pressure cooker and then stir the onion and bell pepper into it. Cook and let the onion cook so it becomes soft, which takes around 5 minutes. After this time add in the garlic and cook a few more minutes.
2. In a small bowl add the water and tomato paste, dissolve, and then pour in with the rest of the ingredients. Place the chicken into the pan and space them out and then add just enough water to cover the chicken.
3. Seal the cooker and bring it to a high pressure before reducing the heat just a bit. Let this cook for about 15 minutes.
4. Turn the heat off and let it drop down naturally for around 20 minutes.
5. Season the chicken with some salt and then serve.

Fenugreek Chicken

Ingredients:
¼ c. oil
1 whole chicken, cut up in 8 pieces
1 tsp. cumin seeds
1 cardamom pod, black
4 green chilies
1 sliced onion
4 cloves, whole
1 Tbsp. garlic and ginger paste
½ c. spinach, chopped
1 Tbsp. fenugreek leaves, dried
½ c. chopped fenugreek leaves, fresh
½ tsp. turmeric
½ tsp. red pepper
1 c. water
½ tsp. Garam masala

Directions:

1. Heat up some oil in the pressure cooker before adding the chicken pieces and brown them on each side, cook for 5 minutes.
2. Take the chicken out of the cooker and place to the side. Add in the chili peppers, garlic and ginger paste, onion slices, cloves, cardamom pod, cinnamon stick, and cumin seeds. Cook for 5 minutes before adding in the rest of the ingredients and cooking for another 5 minutes.
3. Finally, pour the water into the mixture before adding the chicken back in. Bring it all to boil for a few minutes before placing the lid on top of the cooker.
4. Cook this meal for around 30 minutes. Serve with your favorite sides and enjoy.

Giblets

Ingredients:

1 lb. chicken giblets
1 c. flour, all purpose
½ tsp. olive oil
Pepper
Salt
1 chopped onion
½ c. water

Directions:

1. Take out the pressure cooker and rub some oil all over the insides of it. Season the flour with pepper and salt and then dredge the giblets through it to coat.
2. Place the giblets and the onion into the pressure cooker and sauté them a bit before adding in the water.
3. Put the lid on top of the pressure cooker and let it heat up to the proper pressure. Cook the giblets for around 30 minutes so that they are cooked through.
4. Eat these on their own or have with one of your favorite sides.

Hungarian Chicken

Ingredients:
1 Tbsp. vegetable oil
1 chopped onion
4 lbs. chicken legs
2 tsp. hot paprika
1 chopped tomato
½ c. chicken broth
½ c. sour cream
6 oz. cooked egg noodles

Directions:

1. Heat up some oil in the pressure cooker and heat it until it starts to smoke. Add the chicken and let it cook for 5 minutes so it turns golden. Remove from the cooker.
2. Add the broth, paprika, and onion and then stir in order to mix. Place back into the pot and then add on the tomato, but do not stir. Add salt.
3. Lock the lid o and bring the pressure to high and cook for 5 minutes. Reduce the heat and continue to cook for another 7 minutes. After this time remove off heat and allow to finish cooking for another 5 minutes.
4. Slowly release out the pressure and then move the chicken over to a plate. Set it aside but keep warm while the liquid continues to cook in the cooker for another 15 minutes.
5. Bring out a bowl and whisk the sour cream so it becomes smooth. Add in a bit of liquid from the cooker and whisk again.
6. Pour this mixture into the pot before placing the chicken back in and reheat for a few minutes. Salt to taste.
7. Spread out your noodles on a platter and then arrange chicken over it. Pour the sauce on it all and then serve.

Chicken Piccata

Ingredients:

½ c. flour, all purpose
6 chicken breasts
¼ c. olive oil
3 crushed garlic cloves
4 shallots
1/3 c. lemon juice
2 tsp. salt
1 Tbsp. sherry wine
1 tsp. basil
¼ tsp. white pepper
¼ c. sour cream
1 c. pimento olive
1 Tbsp. flour
¼ c. Parmesan cheese
1 lemon sliced

Directions:

1. Dust the pieces of chicken with some flour. Take out the pressure cooker and heat up the oil inside. Add the chicken in and let the pieces sauté in some oil so that it is brown all over and then set aside when done.

2. Add the garlic and shallots into the oil and heat up. Stir in the olives, basil, pepper, salt, sherry, lemon juice, and broth. Mix it together well.

3. Add the chicken back in and then secure the lid. Let the pressure build up to high and then reduce the heat just a bit. Cook the meal for 10 minutes.

4. When this is done, stir the chicken mixture and then move to a serving platter, preserving the heat.

5. In a small bowl, whisk together the flour and sour cream. Stir in a bit of the cooking liquid and then cook for another minute.

Spoon this sauce on the chicken and then sprinkle with the cheese before garnishing with lemon. Serve warm.

Chicken and Green Chili Stew

Ingredients:

1 whole chicken
1 tsp. thyme
1 tsp. cumin
1 tsp. marjoram
1 Tbsp. basil
1 can green chili peppers
1 chopped onion
4 peppers
2 garlic cloves
4 chopped carrots
1 can of stewed tomatoes
5 chopped celery stalks
Salt
Pepper
3 Tbsp. flour, all purpose
3 peeled and cubed potatoes

Directions:

1. Place the chicken into the pressure cover and add enough water in order to cover. Add the basil, marjoram, thyme, and cumin.

2. Bring this to a boil before letting it cook for 45 minutes in the pressure cooker. After this time you can place the chicken back in the pot and add the potatoes, tomatoes, celery, carrots, garlic, onion, and chili peppers.

3. Place the lid on top and let it cook for 10 minutes. While that is cooking, you can bring out a bowl and mix the flour and water. Add this to the soup and stir it well.

4. Raise the heat a bit to finish cooking and then turn the pressure cooker off.

5. Season with some pepper and salt and then taste to serve. Serve with a side of hot, toasted garlic bread to complete the meal.

Kale and Sausage Soup

Ingredients:
2 chopped carrots
1 lb. sausage links
2 chopped onion
2 minced garlic cloves
1 c. Portobello mushroom caps, chopped
6 c. chicken broth
2 c. chopped kale
1 c. cauliflower, chopped
½ tsp. oregano
1 bay leaf

Directions:

1. Bring out the pressure cooker and place the sausage inside. Let it cook for a few minutes in order to cook the sausages. When they are done take out and place on a cooking board in order to cool.
2. Using the reserved drippings of the sausage, place the onion and carrots inside and cook or 5 minutes. Then you can add the garlic and cook for 15 seconds before adding the chicken broth. Bring this to a boil.
3. Return the sausages into the stew and add the oregano, bay leaf, kale, cauliflower, and mushrooms. Place the lid on top and let the pressure build to high.
4. Cook the ingredients for 15 minutes or until sausage is done. At this time take the sausage out, cut it up, and place back into the stew. Simmer an additional 5 minutes before serving.

Ham and Split Pea Soup

Ingredients:

8 c. water
1 lb. split peas, dried
1 ham bone
1 diced onion
2 diced celery ribs
2 diced carrots
Sherry wine
1 ½ tsp. of thyme

Directions:

1. Fill up the pressure cooker with the water and all the ingredients besides the sherry, making sure that the cooker never gets over half full.
2. Place the lid on top of the cooker and then bring it to a high pressure. When you reach the correct pressure, cook the meal for 20 minutes. Let it release the steam naturally.
3. Take the meat out and take it off the bone. Shred it up before placing back into the soup. Add more salt if you like and serve with a bit of Sherry if you would like.

Beef Stew

Ingredients:
½ tsp. salt
¼ c. flour
¼ tsp. dry mustard
1 ½ tsp. olive oil
1 lb. cubed beef
½ c. beef broth
2 Tbsp. garlic, minced
½ c. onion, chopped
2 c. potatoes, diced
1 can of un-drained tomatoes
2 Tbsp. tomato paste
1 Tbsp. brown sugar
2 Tbsp. balsamic vinegar
2 bay leaves
1 ½ tsp. of thyme
Pepper
Salt

Directions:

1. Bring out a bag and mix together the dry mustard, salt, and flour. Add the beef to the bag and then shake in order to coat.
2. Take out your pressure cooker and heat up the oil inside. Put the beef inside and let them brown on all sides. Add in the broth and then bring it to a boil.
3. Add in the rest of the ingredients before putting the lid on top. Bring it to a high pressure and cook he stew for 12 minutes.
4. When this is done, get rid of the pressure, take out the bay leaves, and then serve

Beef Barley and Vegetable Soup

Ingredients:

1 can tomatoes, crushed
1 ¼ lbs. ground beef
2 ½ cups water
3 carrots
½ c. barley
2 celery stalks
1 Idaho potatoes
1 onion
½ tsp. basil
1 garlic clove
½ tsp. thyme
½ tsp. marjoram
½ tsp. rosemary
Pepper & ¼ tsp. kosher salt

Directions:

1. Take out the pressure cooker and brown the beef until it is done. Drain off the fat before adding the barley, water, and tomatoes. Close the cooker and let it get to full pressure. Reduce the heat and then cook for about 10 minutes.
2. While soup is cooking you can split up the carrots before peeling and dicing the potato. Dice onion and mince the garlic as well.
3. Once the soup is done cooking, you can release the pressure before adding pepper, salt, marjoram, rosemary, thyme, basil, and the vegetables.
4. Close the lid again and bring it back up to full pressure. Stabilize the heat and cook for another 10 minutes.
5. Serve the soup right away.

Veggies and Steak

Ingredients:
4 potatoes
1 lb. round steak
3 carrots
2 red peppers
2 green peppers
2 Tbsp. olive oil
8 oz. mushrooms
2 tsp. beef base
2 Tbsp. flour
1 tsp. seasoning
½ tsp. garlic salt
½ garlic powder

Directions:

1. Take all of the fat off the steak. Cut it into cubes and toss with the flour to coat.
2. Heat up the oil in a pan and then brown it up all over. When this is done, place the meat into the cooker.
3. Peel up the potatoes before cutting into cubes and adding to the cooker. Wash and cut up the mushrooms and place into the cooker.
4. Mix some of the beef soup base with water and add into the cooker as well. Cover with the lid and seal. Cook on a high pressure for about 15 minutes.
5. While that is cooking, cut up the carrots and steam it with a cup of water and the rest of the soup base.
6. Cut the peppers as well and add in with the carrots. Steam until they are tender.
7. When the pressure cooker is done, cool it down and then open the lid. Combine the peppers and carrots with the ingredients in the cooker and then serve it all hot. Enjoy!

Meatballs

Ingredients:

2 pieces of whole wheat bread
1 lb. ground beef
½ c. milk
8 oz. pork, ground
1 egg
1 minced onion
1 ½ Tbsp of thyme
½ tsp. salt
1 Tbsp. oregano, dried
¼ c. butter
¾ can chicken stock
¼ c. flour, all purpose
½ c. whipping cream
Pepper and Salt
Egg noodles, cooked
Herbs for garnish

Directions:

1. In a bowl, pour the milk and then soak the bread so that is becomes absorbed. Use your hands to break the bread up before mixing in the pork and beef.

2. Stir in the salt, oregano, thyme, onion, and egg into small balls. Set these aside.

3. Next, bring out the pressure cooker and melt the butter inside. Add the flour and stir so that it becomes moist. Slowly whisk in the water and beef broth and bring this to simmer. Add the meatballs in with the sauce.

4. Place the lid on top and bring the cooker to full pressure. Reduce the heat a bit and then cook for about 10 minutes.

5. When this is done cooking, remove the cooker from the heat and let the pressure out quickly.

6. Add in the cream and simmer for a few minutes to get the sauce to thicken. Serve warm with the prepared egg noodles and garnish of your choice.

Cheese and Potato Soup

Ingredients:

4 chopped onions
4 cubed potatoes
2 tsp. salt
4 c. milk
1 ½ cups of water
3 c. grated cheddar cheese
¼ tsp. pepper
1 Tbsp. chopped parsley

Directions:

1. Take out the pressure cooker and place the water, salt, onions, and potatoes inside. Close the cooker and bring it to full pressure. Reduce the heat and then cook for another 3 minutes. Remove from the heat.
2. Give the cooker time to cool down so that there isn't any pressure inside before opening. Mix this mixture in a blender until it is smooth before placing back into the cooker.
3. Add the pepper and milk inside and then turn the cooker on so that it begins to boil. Add the cheese and stir so that is can melt.
4. Serve right away and enjoy.

Clam Chowder

Ingredients:
3 cans minced clams
½ lb. bacon, lean
3 c. diced and peeled potatoes
¼ tsp. white pepper
1 tsp. salt
2 Tbsp. butter
2 c. milk
2 c. half and half
Pinch thyme
Pinch Paprika

Directions:

1. Darin out the clams, but make sure to reserve the liquid. Add enough of the water in order to have 4 cups altogether.
2. Take out the pressure cooker and brown up the bacon so it turns golden. Take the bacon out and set it aside.
3. Drain off most of the fat, but leave a little in order to sauté the onion for a few minutes. Add in the reserved clam and water mixture as well as the pepper, salt, and potatoes and bring to boil.
4. Seal the cooker and raise the pressure before reducing the heat and cooking for about 10 minutes.
5. After his time you can take from the heat, depressurize the cooker and take the heat off.
6. Add in the clams, butter, milk, and half and half. Heat up a bit before serving.

Italian Potato Soup

Ingredients:
6 sliced leeks
¼ c. olive oil
2 carrots
3 cubed potatoes
½ c. Arborio rice
5 c. chicken stock
½ c. chopped celery
½ c. chopped parsley
¼ tsp. pepper & 1 tsp. salt
2 Tbsp. lemon juice
2 tsp. basil
3 Tbsp. tomato paste
10 oz. spinach
1 Tbsp. brown sugar
¼ c. grated Parmesan
¼ c. grated fontinella cheese

Directions:

1. Take out the pressure cooker and heat the oil inside. Add in the carrots, garlic, and leeks and let it sauté for 2 minutes.
2. Add the potatoes and rice to this and cook for another minute. After this time add in the brown sugar, tomato paste, lemon juice, basil, pepper, salt, bay leaf, celery, parsley, and broth.
3. Place the lid on the cooker and let it build up to high pressure. Reduce the heat a bit and cook the meal for 4 minutes.
4. After this time you can release the pressure and then take the lid off. Stir the soup well before ladling into a few bowls.
5. Combine the cheeses before sprinkling onto the soup and serving with some Italian bread.

Lamb Stew

Ingredients:
1 Tbsp. olive oil
1 Tbsp. garlic, minced
2 sliced onion
¼ c. red wine vinegar
14 oz. chopped tomatoes
2 lbs. lamb shoulder cubes
2 Tbsp. tomato paste
1 tsp. oregano
1 tsp. basil
2 bay leaves
1 red bell pepper
1/3 minced parsley
1 green bell pepper

Directions:

1. Place some oil into the pressure cooker. Add the garlic and onions and sauté for 2 minutes so that the onions can become soft.
2. Add the vinegar and cook for another 2 minutes. After this time add in the pepper, salt, bay leaves, oregano, basil, tomato paste, tomatoes, and lamb. Stir it well to blend.
3. Place the lid on and turn on a high heat to get a high pressure. Cook for 12 minutes. When this is done allow the pressure to drop and cook for another 10 minutes.
4. Take the lid off and allow the excess heat to leave.
5. Remove the bay leaves and add in the peppers.
6. Cover the cooker again and simmer for an addition 8 minutes so that the peppers can cook a bit.
7. Stir the parsley in and add more seasonings if you would like. Serve with some noodles and enjoy.

Chili

Ingredients:
2 tsp. peanut oil
3 lbs. meat of choice
1 ½ tsp. salt
1 container salsa
1 bottle beer
30 tortilla chips
1 Tbsp. adobo sauce
2 chipotle chilies
1 Tbsp. tomato paste
1 tsp. cumin
1 Tbsp. chili powder

Directions:

1. Take the meat and place it into a mixing bowl. Add the salt and peanut oil, toss, and then set aside.
2. Bring out a pressure cook and heat it up until it is hot. Add in the meat, in batches if you need, and brown it all over for about 2 minutes on each batch. Once the batch is browned, place into a bowl and work on the other one.
3. Once it is all done, add the beer into the cooker and use it to deglaze the pot. Scrape the browned bits to the bottom before adding the meat back into the cooker.
4. Add ground cumin, chili powder, tomato paste, adobo sauce, chipotle peppers, chips, & salsa, stir to combine.
5. Put the lid on top and then let the pressure go until it is high. Cook this for about 25 minutes before removing from the heat. Slowly release the steam from the pressure cooker.
6. Serve this meal right away and enjoy!

Beef Recipes

Cabbage and Corned Beef

Ingredients:
4 c. water
3 quartered garlic cloves
2 bay leaves
2 ½ lbs. corned beef brisket
4 carrots
1 head cabbage
3 quartered turnips
6 quartered potatoes
Horseradish sauce

Directions:

1. Pour some water into the pressure cooker. Add in the brisket and heat it up so that the water is at a rolling boil. Skim the fat from the surface.
2. At this time add in the bay leaves and garlic before placing the lid on top. Heat up the cooker to a high pressure. Reduce the heat a bit and then cook for an hour and fifteen minutes.
3. Take the lid off slowly at this time and then add in the vegetables. Place the lid back on and get it back up to a high pressure. Reduce the heat a bit again and cook for another 6 minutes.
4. Remove the lid and then serve with some horseradish sauce.

Pot Roast

Ingredients:
3 lbs. chuck roast
1 Tbsp. olive oil
1 Tbsp. salt
1 c. peeled carrots
1 c. sliced onion
1 c. chopped celery
1¾ c. water
5 peeled and cut potatoes
¼ c. Worcestershire sauce
½ tsp. pepper
2 bay leaves
2 tsp. beef base

Directions:

1. Use the season all salt in order to coat the roast all over. Use a pan or the base of the pressure cooker to brown your meat with the olive oil so that the juices are seared in. Add the onions, celery, and carrots when the meat is almost done. In the end, add the Worcestershire sauce and water.
2. Place this mixture along with the potato halves into the pressure cooker. Add the bay leaves, beef base, and pepper.
3. Lock the cooker lid on top and then bring it to a high pressure. Stabilize the pressure and then cook the roast for an hour.
4. When it is done, release the pressure. Test the meat to see that it is done. If not, add in some water and return to high pressure.
5. When you are done, release the pressure before serving warm.

Beef Curry

Ingredients:

1 jar curry paste
1 can of coconut milk
1 Tbsp. olive oil
2 quartered onions
1 Tbsp. brown sugar
1 c. water
1 red bell pepper
1 Tbsp. soy sauce
1 tsp. salt
3 lbs. chuck roast
1 Tbsp. fish sauce
4 potatoes
1 c. rice
2 Tbsp. basil

Directions:

1. Cut the meat up so that it is in small sections, getting rid of any fat. Chop up the onions and bell pepper.

2. Brown the peppers and onion in the oil until one of the sides are charred in the pressure cooker. Take the vegetables out and work on the curry sauce. To do this, add the cream from the milk to the pan and deglaze.

3. Add all of the curry paste and mix it well. Cook for 5 minutes, making sure to stir often. Add in the rest of the milk, water, and the other ingredients and mix well.

4. Dump the potatoes, vegetables, and beef in as well.

5. Place the rice and some water into a bowl and cover with a lid. Place over the curry to cook up.

6. Bring this to a high pressure and cook the meal for about 12 minutes. When this is done you can release the pressure.

7. Take the lid off and then remove the rice bowl. Put some into a bowl and then top with the veggies, meat, and curry. Serve warm.

Beef Tips and Rice

Ingredients:
3 Tbsp. flour, all purpose
2 tsp. salt
½ tsp. paprika
½ tsp. pepper
¼ tsp. mustard powder
2 Tbsp. vegetable oil
2 lbs. sirloin steaks, cubed
2 chopped onions
2 minced garlic cloves
4 c. rice, cooked
1 can beef consommé

Directions:

1. Place the five first ingredients into a plastic bag and then shake them well. Add in the cubes of beef in the bag and then shake until they are covered well.
2. Bring out your pressure cooker and place the oil with the meat inside. Brown the meat on all sides.
3. Once this is done, add in the garlic and onions and let them sauté while you are deglazing the pan. When the onions are done, add the beef consommé and then stir to mix.
4. Put the lid on top of the cooker before turning on high pressure. Cook the meal for 25 minutes. Take off the heat.
5. When the pressure is gone, open up the lid and then simmer the meal so that it reaches the right consistency.
6. Serve the beef tips on your cooked rice.

Chicago Steak Roll

Ingredients:
1 c. flour
2 ½ lbs. round steak
½ tsp. pepper & 1 tsp. salt
1 ¼ c. onions, chopped
1 c. breadcrumbs
2 c. butternut squash, chopped
¼ c. green pepper chopped
¼ c. celery, chopped
1 beaten egg
¼ c. butter
2 Tbsp. melted butter
1 c. water

Directions:
1. Take the meat and cut it up in 8 pieces. Pound each of the pieces so they are ¼ an inch thick.
2. In a bowl you can combine the pepper, salt, and flour. Dredge the pieces of meat through this flour mixture.
3. In another bowl, mix the melted butter, egg, some salt, celery, green pepper, squash, onion, and bread crumbs together. Spread this out over each of the meat pieces and then roll them up. Fasten using a toothpick.
4. Bring out the pressure cooker and place the meat rolls and the butter inside. Brown the meat on all sides before removing from the pan.
5. Place a steamer basket and water into the pressure cooker. Place the rolls into the basket and then close the top of the cooker well.
6. Cook this for 15 minutes at a high pressure. When this is done, cool down the cooker right away.

Take the beef out and serve with the sauces as gravy. Enjoy.

Vietnamese Pho Bo

Ingredients:

2 lbs. beef bones
1 ginger piece
1 lb. beef brisket
4 star anise
1 onion
6 cloves
10 c. water
1 cinnamon stick
3 Tbsp. fish sauce
1 tsp. salt
1 Tbsp. pepper
1 tsp. sugar
2 c. bean sprouts
2 sliced spring onions
1 lime
1 sliced chili pepper
1 basil bunch
300 g. rice noodles

Directions:

1. Peel the onion and ginger and then char them under the broiler so that they become well blackened. Set this aside.
2. Take out the pressure cooker and brown up the meat in batches in order to get a good color. Set this aside.
3. Clean the pot out before placing the water, cinnamon, cloves, anise, onion, ginger, and meat inside. Set on the high heat.
4. Bring the ingredients to a boil before skimming the scum from the top. Close the cooker and let it get to a high pressure. Reduce the heat and cooking for about 50 minutes.

5. When this time is done, release the pressure and skim fat from the stock. Add the pepper, sugar, salt, and fish sauce to the cooker and bring it back up to a boil.
6. Add in the noodles and cook for a few more minutes so that they become soft.
7. Serve this really hot with the rest of the ingredients on the side.

Barbecue Spareribs

Ingredients:

10 lbs. spareribs cut up
Paprika
Salt
Pepper
3 tsp. vegetable oil
4 sliced onion
1 c. vinegar
2 c. ketchup
2 tsp. Worcestershire sauce
1 tsp. celery seed
1 tsp. chili powder

Directions:

1. Take the ribs and season with the paprika, pepper, and salt.
2. Heat up the pressure cooker before adding in some oil and heating up. Brown the ribs on all sides before adding the onions.
3. When the meat is browned you can combine the rest of the ingredients into a bowl and then pour on top of the ribs.
4. Close the lid of the cooker securely and then turn on a high pressure. Cook the meal for 15 minutes.
5. Allow the pressure to drop off after this time before taking the lid off. Serve with your favorite vegetables and enjoy.

Baby Back Ribs

Ingredients:

3 lbs. beef back ribs
¼ tsp. pepper
½ tsp. salt
½ tsp. onion powder
¼ tsp. garlic powder
½ tsp. onion powder
¼ tsp. paprika
1 c. beer
12 oz. BBQ sauce

Directions:

1. Cut up the ribs so they are in serving pieces. Mix the spices together in a bowl to make a rub. Apply this rub all over the ribs.
2. Bring out the pressure cooker and heat up the oil inside. Add the ribs and let them brown on all the sides.
3. Insert a cooking rack into the cooker before adding the beer. Load the rack with the ribs, making sure to not go over the fill line.
4. Place the lid on top and get it to a high pressure. Reduce the heat a bit and cook the ribs for 35 minutes.
5. When this is done, allow the cooker to depressurize naturally. Take the rack out of the cooker before adding in the BBQ sauce. Heat so that it can simmer.
6. Cook for another 15 minutes. Serve warm.

Beef Stroganoff

Ingredients:
1 lb. beef chunk, stew
1 chopped onion
1 tsp. nutmeg
1 Tbsp. oil
1 minced garlic clove
1 Tbsp. Dijon mustard
Pepper
1 can of sliced mushrooms
1 ½ tsp. beef bouillon
1 c. water
½ tsp. salt
¼ c. water
1 container sour cream
2 Tbsp. cornstarch
Noodles, cooked

Directions:

1. Take out the slow cooker and place your first 11 ingredients inside. Place the lid on top and let this simmer for 20 minutes at a high pressure before taking from the heat.
2. Once the pressure goes away, take the lid off and stir the sour cream into your broth.
3. Take out a bowl and stir together the cornstarch and water. Add this into the simmering broth slowly, making sure to stir often.
4. When it is warmed up, serve over the cooked noodles and then enjoy.

Beef Ribs

Ingredients:

2 ½ c. beef broth
3 Tbsp. oil
¾ c. steak sauce
10 dashes Worcestershire
2 tsp. mesquite marinade, dry
1 diced sweet onion
1 tsp. steak seasoning
3 Tbsp. minced garlic
½ tsp. mesquite smoke, liquid
5 lbs. beef ribs

Directions:

1. Take the salt and pepper and season the ribs with it.
2. Heat up the pressure cooker and then place the oil inside. Add in the ribs and then brown them on all sides.
3. In a bowl combine all of the rest of the ingredients together until well mixed. Pour this all over the ribs.
4. Place the lid on top and let the pressure heat up to high. Cook for 7 minutes. After this time allow the pressure to drop down on its own.
5. Crisp up the ribs for a few minutes and then add on a little BBQ sauce before serving.

Veal Brisket

Ingredients:
3 lbs. veal
½ c. flour
3 Tbsp. olive oil
3 shallots
1 sweet onion
1 tsp. thyme
6 garlic cloves
½ tsp. pepper
½ tsp. salt
½ c. red wine
2 c. beef broth

Directions:
1. Bring out the veal and trim off the fat. Chop up the onions, garlic, and shallots before setting aside.
2. Place the flour in a bowl and dredge the brisket through it.
3. Heat up some oil in a pan and place the brisket inside. Brown all over and then set aside. You will also be able to do this in the pressure cooker if you would like.
4. Using the same pan, place the shallots, onions, and garlic inside. Sauté so that they become browned.
5. Take all of the ingredients and place them inside the pressure cooker. Put the lid on top and cook at a high pressure or 45 minutes.
6. After this time is done, turn the heat off and open up the cooker.
7. Remove the brisket and slice it up. Return your slices to the cooker with the gravy.
8. Serve this over some noodles or rice.

Beef and Noodles

Ingredients:

1 chopped onion
3 lbs. chuck roast, boneless
1 minced garlic clove
Pepper
Salt
2 Tbsp. vegetable oil
1 c. water
Mashed potatoes
8 oz. egg noodles

Directions:

1. Cut up the roast into smaller pieces. Place into the cooker with some oil and brown the meat. Add in the pepper, salt, garlic, and onion to the meat as well as some water.
2. Close the cooker with the lid, turn on to a high pressure, and let it cook for about 35 minutes.
3. When it is done, lower the pressure naturally. Take the lid off the cooker and remove the meat. Add in some more water and then bring it up to boil.
4. When the liquid is warmed up, add the noodles and cook for another 9 minutes so they become tender.
5. Lower the heat and add in some more water if it is needed. The broth will be able to thicken during this time to make the gravy.
6. Once the noodles are tender, place the meat back into the cooker and serve warm.

New England Cider Pot Roast

Ingredients:

2 Tbsp. light molasses
2 c. apple cider
2 tsp. salt
½ tsp. peppercorns
8 berries, allspice
2 minced garlic cloves
½ tsp. ginger
4 quartered onions
6 lb. chuck roast, beef
4 chopped celery stalks
¼ c. butter
3 Tbsp. water
3 Tbsp. cornstarch

Directions:

1. Take out a bowl and combine the ginger, garlic, peppercorns, allspice, salt, molasses, and apple cider together.
2. In another dish, place the celery, onions, and beef inside and then pour the mixture all over the meat. Place into the fridge and let it marinade for 24 hours.
3. When you are ready to cook it, take the meat out of the sauce and then wipe dry.
4. Heat up some butter in a skillet. Add in the pot roast and let it brown on all sides.
5. Take the pressure cooker out and add the trivet inside. Place the meat on the trivet and pour the vegetables and marinade all over it. Bring the mixture to a boil.
6. Seal up the cooker and let it get up to a high pressure. Reduce the heat a bit to stabilize and then let the meat cook for an hour.

7. After this time, take the cooker off the heat and let the pressure release. Strain the vegetables and meat out, making sure to save the juices.
8. Place the reserved juices back into the cooker and let them boil. Mix together the cornstarch with some water before adding in with the juices and allowing it to thicken.
9. Add in some more seasonings if you would like.
10. Slice the meat before serving with the juices and enjoy.

Beef Bourguignon

Ingredients:
4 peeled and cut carrots
1 ½ lbs. chuck roast, beef
2 ¾ c. halved mushrooms
2 minced garlic cloves
¾ c. onion
¾ tsp. salt
1 bay leaf
¼ tsp. pepper
½ tsp. crushed thyme
2/3 c. beef broth
¼ c. water
2 Tbsp. tomato paste
2/3 c. dry red wine
2 Tbsp. four
6 c. egg noodles, cooked

Directions:
1. Bring out the pressure cooker and then combine the tomato paste, wine, beef broth, pepper, thyme, salt, bay leaf, garlic, onion, mushrooms, carrots, and beef together inside.
2. Place the lid on the cooker and then lock it into place. Bring the pressure up and then reduce it just a bit. Cook the meal for about 12 minutes.
3. After this time, take the cooker off the heat and let the pressure come back down. When it is down, unlock the lid and take it off.
4. Take the bay leaf out of the cooker. Take out a bowl and combine the water and flour before adding into the cooker.
5. Turn the heat back up to medium and continue to cook so the stew becomes thick and bubbly.
6. Take the cooker off the heat and then serve this on top of egg noodles to enjoy.

Italian Beef

Ingredients

3 tsp. cooking oil
9 lbs. rump steak
3 chopped onions
2 c. celery, diced
3 bay leaves
3 chopped carrots
1 tsp. salt
3 cans tomato paste
2 c. mushrooms, sliced
2 cans beef broth
1 ½ c. red wine, dry

Directions:

1. Heat up the cooker before adding the oil inside. When the oil is warm, add in the roast and let it brown all over. After this is done, add the seasonings and the veggies.
2. Blend the broth, wine, and paste together before pouring this mixture all over the vegetables and meat.
3. Cover up the pressure cooker and then turn it up to a high pressure. Cook the meal for 35 minutes.
4. When the cooking is done, drop the pressure down naturally. Thicken up the gravy by cooking for a few more minutes and then serve.

Tex Mex Brisket

Ingredients:
3 minced garlic cloves
1 minced onion
1 serrano chili
1 Tbsp. chili powder
1 ½ Tbsp. brown sugar
1 Tbsp. apple cider vinegar
1 tsp. salt
½ tsp. cumin
3 lbs. trimmed beef brisket
1/8 tsp. pepper
1 onion
14 oz. diced tomatoes
2 Tbsp. vegetable oil

Directions:
1. Combine together the salt, cumin, vinegar, chili powder, sugar, chili, garlic, and onion in a bowl and mix together.
2. Use this mixture to rub on the brisket before moving over to a dish. Cover and allow it to marinate like this for 24 hours.
3. When you are ready to cook, heat up the oil in a pressure cooker. Turn on to a high setting before placing the meat inside. Without covering the cooker, cook the meat for 8 minutes to brown all over.
4. After this time, add in the tomatoes, making sure to get some under the meat. Add in the onion wedges.
5. Cover the cooker and turn it on to a high pressure. Stabilize the pressure and then cook the meal for an hour.
6. When it is done, release the pressure and then remove the lid. Slice up the meat. Serve this with the pan juice and enjoy.

Bison Meatloaf

Ingredients:

1 chopped onion
2 lbs. buffalo meat
3 chopped celery stalks
1 tsp. salt
3 Tbsp. Italian seasoning
¼ c. ketchup
1 tsp. salt
1 c. breadcrumbs
½ c. shredded cheese
1 egg

Directions:

1. To start this, bring out a food processor and throw everything inside. Combine well. Form this mixture into a loaf.
2. In a skillet you should brown the loaf all over. Cut it in half and then put inside a pressure cooker.
3. Add just enough water in order to be over the meatloaf. Put the lid on top of the cooker and then cook on a high pressure for about 15 minutes.
4. When the meal is done, take the loaf out of the cooker and drizzle the top with ketchup before serving.

Swiss Steak

Ingredients:

¼ c. flour
3 lbs. round steak
Salt
Pepper
½ chopped onion
1 tsp. cooking oil
1 chopped green pepper
1 c. tomato juice

Directions:

1. Take the flour and place it into a bowl. Season with some pepper and salt before pounding this mixture into the beef.
2. Heat up the pressure cooker. Add in the oil and the steaks and brown them on all sides. At this time you can add in the rest of the ingredients and place the lid on top of the pressure cooker.

Turn this on to high heat and cook for 15 minutes. When the meal is done cooking, allow the pressure to drop down naturally and then serve this warm.

Pork Recipes

Pork Chops

Ingredients:

1 c. corn flake crumbs, crushed
Pepper
Salt
5 pork chops
1 beaten egg
3 Tbsp. oil
1Tbsp. milk
½ c. water

Directions:

1. Take the pepper and salt and season the pork chops with them. When this is done, dredge the pork chops with the corn flakes.
2. Combine the milk and the egg and then dip the pork chops into it before dredging through the crumbs again.
3. Bring out the pressure cooker and place the shortening inside. Add the chops and brown on all sides.
4. When browned, add the water and then close the lid on securely. Heat up the pressure and cook for 12 minutes.
5. After the meal is done, allow the pressure to drop down naturally before serving with your favorite vegetables.

Pork Loin

Ingredients:
32 oz. chicken broth
4 lbs. pork loin
¼ c. oil
1 quartered onion
2 crushed garlic cloves
3 Tbsp. cold water
3 Tbsp. Italian seasoning
3 Tbsp. cornstarch

Directions:
1. Get the pork loin ready. To do this, you can season with the garlic and Italian seasoning.
2. Heat up some oil in the cooker and then place in some of the onion pieces. Cook for a few minutes before taking the onions out.
3. Place the roast into the cooker and then brown all over. Take the roast out of the cooker and then add in the chicken broth, making sure to scrape the bottoms of the cooker in order to get the bits out.
4. Add the roast and the onion back in and then cook for about an hour. After this time you can remove the cooker from the heat, allowing the pressure to go down naturally.
5. Then take the onions and roast out and put onto a serving dish. Tent with foil and allow to rest, for about 15 minutes.
6. While that is cooling, bring out a bowl and mix the corn starch and water together. Add in the rest of the broth and then bring up the liquid to a boil. Add in the cornstarch mixture to the cooker.
7. Take the cooker form the heat and then pour this liquid out over the roast before serving.

Pork Bone Spaghetti

Ingredients:

2 jars spaghetti sauce
3 lbs. pork bones
1 lbs. pasta
Water
Cheese

Directions:

1. Take out the pressure cooker and place the water and the neck bones inside. Turn it on and allow to steam. Cook for about 30 minutes. Do this to remove the fat off the bones.
2. Take the liquid around the bones out of the cooker and then pour the spaghetti sauce inside.
3. Bring this to simmering, making sure to stir often so nothing sticks to the bottom.
4. When this is done, serve with the prepared pasta and then top with cheese before serving.

Pork Ragu

Ingredients:

2 lbs. cubed stew meat, pork
¼ c. diced pancetta
1 diced yellow onion
1 diced carrot
1 c. red wine
3 minced garlic cloves
1 can of tomato sauce
1 bay leaf
2 tsp. Italian seasoning
Salt
Pepper

Directions:

1. Take out a cooker and brown up the pork and the pancetta. When they are done you can drain out any extra fat before adding the garlic, carrots, and onions. Cook these for 2 minutes.
2. After this time you can stir the wine in and then boil so half of it evaporates. Scrape up the brown bits from the cooker before adding the pepper, salt, and Italian seasoning. Pour the tomato sauce over the meat.
3. Place the lid on top, without locking it, and then bring the cooker to a high pressure. When it reaches the pressure, reduce the heat a bit and then cook the meal for 8 minutes.
4. Turn the heat off and let the pressure naturally go down. When the pressure is done you can take the lid off and let the steam escape.
5. Take out the bay leaf and then stir. Break the meat up with a spoon and then serve this over polenta, pasta, or rice.

Baja Pork Chops

Ingredients:

¾ c. chili sauce
2 Tbsp. Worcestershire sauce
2 Tbsp. Dijon mustard
1 minced chipotle pepper
2 lbs. pork chops without bones
1 Tbsp. maple syrup
1 Tbsp. adobo sauce
1 Tbsp. olive oil
2 diced green peppers
2 c. chopped onions
½ c. water
2 lbs. red potatoes
Salt
Pepper

Directions:

1. Take out a bowl and blend the maple syrup, Worcestershire, mustard, and chili sauce. Add in the pork and then toss to coat. Put this into the fridge and allow the pork to marinade for about 2 hours.

2. When you are ready to cook, heat up the oil in a pressure cooker before adding the onions. Cook the onions for 2 minutes. Add in the peppers and continue cooking for an additional minute.

3. Add the water. Place some of the potatoes in the bottom before adding in the pork and leftover marinade to the cooker, but do not stir.

4. Add in the rest of the potatoes on top before locking the lid over the cooker. Bring it up to a high pressure. Reduce the heat a bit and then cook the meal for 12 minutes. Use a quick release method to end the cooking process.

5. Take the lid off and test to see if the meal is done. If it needs a few more minutes, return the cooker to a high pressure.

6. Serve this meal warm.

Pork and Gravy

Ingredients:
1 chopped onion
¼ c. tarragon Dijon mustard
1 Tbsp. oil
Pepper
Salt
1 c. water
3 lbs. pork loin chops, boneless
2 Tbsp. flour

Directions:

1. Season the pork chops using the pepper and salt. Place some of the oil in the frying pan and then add the chops. Brown on all sides in order to sear the juices. Take from the heat.
2. Add in some more oil to your pressure cooker and place the onions inside. Sauté this so it becomes caramelized. When this is done, add a cup of water.
3. Take the meat and add it into the cooker. Spread out the mustard all over the chops inside the cooker and add the lid on top.
4. Cook at a high pressure for about 30 minutes or until it is as tender as you like.
5. When you are done, take the meat out of the cooker. Add in the flour and thicken to finish of the gravy.
6. Serve the chops with the gravy and your favorite side and enjoy.

Vienna Ribs

Ingredients:

2 lbs. pork ribs
Salt
¼ c. mustard
1 tsp. pepper
1 Tbsp. olive oil
1 tsp. paprika
1 sliced onion
1 c. water

Directions:

1. Take each piece of meat and rub it with the mustard all over. Sprinkle with the paprika, pepper, and salt.
2. Put the meat into the pressure cooker and brown it all over. When done, take out of the cooker and drain off for about 2 minutes. Return the ribs to the cooker when they are done draining.
3. Add in the onion and the water before covering the cooker. Turn on to a high pressure and let it cook for about 15 minutes. When done, allow the pressure to drop normally.
4. Serve the prepared ribs over some rice and then enjoy.

BBQ Pork Sandwiches

Ingredients:

6 lbs. pork
1 green onion
¼ c. butter
1 onion
1 tsp. salt
¼ c. sugar
2 tsp. paprika
1 tsp. Worcestershire sauce
3 c. ketchup
2 cans tomato sauce
1 c. cider vinegar
2 tsp. dry mustard
2 tsp. celery seeds
½ tsp. pepper

Directions:

1. Place some butter into a pot and sauté the onions inside. Mix in the rest of the ingredients and let it all simmer for a few hours, making sure to stir a few times.
2. While this is being prepared, place the pork into the pressure cooker. Cook it for around 2 hours or until it begins to fall apart.
3. After this time, take out of the cooker and allow it to cool before shredding with your hands.
4. When ready to serve, place a lot of meat onto a bun before topping with the prepared sauce. Enjoy.

Lemon Pork Chops

Ingredients:

1/8 c. cooking oil
8 pork chops
8 lemon slices
½ tsp. salt
1 ½ onion
½ tsp. pepper
1 c. water
1 c. ketchup

Directions:

1. Bring out the pressure cooker and let it heat up with some oil. Add in the chops and brown them on all sides.
2. When the chops are browned you can top each with a slice of lemon and then add the pepper, salt, and onions to the cooker.
3. Combine the water and ketchup in a bowl and then pour this mixture on top. Place the lid on top of the cooker and close it securely.
4. Turn on the cooker and let it reach a high pressure. Cook the meal for ten minutes.
5. When this is done, allow the pressure to drop down and take the meat out of the cooker. Serve with your favorite side and enjoy.

Pork Stew

Ingredients:
1 ½ lbs. trimmed pork loin
1 c. black beans, dried
1 sliced onion
1 Tbsp. olive oil
2 tsp. garlic, minced
¾ c. orange juice
2 Tbsp. Dijon mustard
½ c. brown sugar
3 peeled and cubed sweet potatoes

Directions:
1. In a pan, place the beans and some water inside. Allow to boil on a high heat for 3 minutes. When this is done take it from the heat and let the beans soak in the water for a minimum of an hour. Drain out the water and rinse.
2. Take the pork and cut it up in 6 slices and cut the slices in half.
3. Sauté the garlic, onion, and pork inside the pressure cooker with the oil. Do this until the meat browns which will take around 10 minutes.
4. Stir the beans as well of the rest ingredients, excluding the sweet potatoes. Close the lid and cook at a high pressure for 12 minutes.
5. When this is done you can cool down the cooker and open up the lid. Add the sweet potatoes before closing the lid and cooking at a high pressure again for another 3 minutes.
6. Cool the cooker again and then serve the stew.

Chickpea Curry

Ingredients:
4 tsp. cumin seeds
8 tsp. olive oil
1 sliced onion
2 tsp. coriander
4 tsp. garlic, crushed
2 tsp. Garam Masala
3 c. chickpeas, cooked
2 tsp. turmeric
2 cans diced tomatoes
¼ tsp. salt and ¼ tsp. pepper
3 peeled and cubed potatoes
½ c. water
Cilantro stem

Directions:
1. Take out the slow cooker and heat up the oil. When it is heated up, cook the cumin for 30 seconds so they begin to crackle. Add in the onion next and stir for another 5 minutes to make it soft and golden.
2. Reduce the heat a bit and stir the garlic with the rest of the spices. Add the rest of the ingredients except the garnish.
3. Close the lid and lock it up. Bring the dish to a high pressure and cook for about 15 minutes.
4. When the meal is done you can release the pressure. Serve the dish with the coriander and parsley. Serve with some rice or another side that you enjoy.

Parsley Fettuccine

Ingredients:

½ lb. pasta, fettuccine
2 Tbsp. olive oil
3 c. water
¼ tsp. pepper, white
1 tsp. salt
½ tsp. crushed summer savory
¼ c. chopped parsley
¼ c. softened butter
¼ c. grated fontinella cheese

Directions:

1. Take out the pressure cooker and heat up the oil. Stir the noodles in with the oil before adding the savory, pepper, salt, and water. Place the lid on top.
2. Turn on to a high pressure to develop steam. Reduce the heat a bit and then cook the meal for 8 minutes.
3. When this is done, release the pressure and take the lid off.
4. Bring out a colander and drain out the noodles. Put back into the cooker. Add in the parsley and the butter and mix so that the noodles can become coated.

Pour this out into a bowl and sprinkle with some cheese before serving

Cuban Red Beans

Ingredients:

1 Tbsp. olive oil
1 bag kidney beans, dried
½ chopped onion
2 Tbsp. chopped garlic
½ chopped green pepper
1 can of tomato sauce
2 chopped carrots
2 chopped potatoes
1 cup vegetable broth
1 dash salt
Pepper
Oregano

Directions:

1. Place the beans into a bowl of water and let them soak for about 12 hours.
2. When you are ready to cook the meal, add some oil to a pressure cooker. Add in the onion, bell pepper, and garlic before adding in the tomato sauce and vegetable broth.
3. Add in the seasonings, carrots, potatoes, and beans to the cooker as well. Add in some more broth to cover it all.
4. Place the lid on the cooker and then bring up to a high pressure. Cook this for 25 minutes.
5. Serve warm.

Macaroni and Cheese

Ingredients:

2 c. chicken stock
2 ½ c. elbow macaroni
1 c. heavy cream
1 tsp. pepper
1 tsp. salt
1 Tbsp. butter
1 ½ c. shredded cheese
½ c. milk
1 ½ c. mozzarella cheese, shredded

Directions:

1. Take out a pressure cooker and place the pepper, salt, cream, chicken stock, and macaroni inside.
2. Turn the cooker on to a high pressure. When it reaches the pressure adjust the heat a bit. Cook this for 7 minutes.
3. Take the cooker from the heat and slowly let the pressure out. Remove lid and get the steam to let out.
4. At this time add in the cheeses, milk, and butter to the pot and stir.
5. Serve this warm.

Quinoa Pilaf

Ingredients:

1 c. peas
1 ½ c. quinoa
¼ tsp. chopped ginger
10 cashew nuts
10 curry leaves
1 sliced red chili pepper
1 onion
1 Tbsp. vegetable oil
2 ½ c. of water
1 Tbsp. lemon juice
1 tsp. seasoning salt

Directions:

1. Take out the pressure cooker and place all of your ingredients inside. Stir to mix once.
2. Place the lid on top on top and cook the meal for about 10 minutes. Take the cooker from the heat when done and reduce the pressure for a few minutes before opening the lid.
3. Garnish the dish with some coriander leaves and serve with chutney and hot.

Cheesy Shells

Ingredients:
¼ c. minced basil
¼ c. minced parsley
1 egg
2 grated garlic cloves
¼ tsp. pepper
½ tsp. salt
1 oz. Romano cheese
1 pinch nutmeg, grated
¼ lb. shredded mozzarella cheese
1 container ricotta cheese
½ c. water
1 jar tomato sauce
6 oz. pasta shells, jumbo

Directions:
1. Beat the egg inside a bowl before adding the ricotta, mozzarella, Romano cheese, nutmeg, pepper, salt, garlic, basil, and parsley. Stir in order to combine.
2. Pour 1/3 of the jar of sauce into the pressure cooker and add some water. Fill pasta shells with the filling you made.
3. Lay out the shells in one layer in the pressure cooker. Cover with the rest of the sauce, making sure that the shells are completely covered.
4. Turn on the cooker and bring the pressure to a high heat and cook for 12 minutes.
5. When it is done, release pressure and then take the lid off. Serve the noodles warm.

Three Bean Salad

Ingredients:

1 c. canned, drained, red kidney beans
1 c. chickpeas beans
1 ½ c. green beans
1 crushed garlic cloves
1 bay leaf

Dressing
½ chopped red onion
2 chopped celery stalks
1 chopped parsley
5 Tbsp. apple cider vinegar
4 Tbsp. olive oil
1 Tbsp. white sugar
Pepper
Salt

Directions:

1. Wrap up the green beans in some foil. Take out the pressure cooker and add in 4 cups of water. Add in the chickpeas, garlic clove, and bay leaf.
2. Place the steamer basket and place the kidney beans inside. Add in the green beans.
3. Use another trivet in order to make sure that the packet stays above the kidney beans.
4. Close the pressure cooker and lock it. Turn the heat to a high pressure and then reduce a bit once the pressure is reached. Cook for 15 minutes.
5. When this time is up, release the pressure and then move the cooker to a cool burner.

6. While the beans cook you can work on the dressing. Cut up the onion and mix into a bowl with the sugar and vinegar. Set aside.
7. When the beans are done, open the green beans. Pour the ones from the basket and the bottom of the cooker into the strainer and rinse to stop the cooking. Slice into pieces and mix together with other beans.
8. Take out a serving bowl and combine the olive oil, parsley, celery, onion, and beans. Add some pepper and salt. Serve right away.

Vegetarian Chili

Ingredients:
500 g. kidney beans
1 ½ liters of water
Vegetables
4 onions
1 can diced tomatoes
2 celery ribs
8 garlic cloves
Seasoning
3 Tbsp. chili powder
¼ c. olive oil
2 Tbsp. cumin powder
1 Tbsp. basil
1 Tbsp. dry oregano
½ tsp. paprika
2 tsp. coriander
¼ tsp. black pepper
1 c. water
1/8 tsp. hot pepper flakes

Directions:
1. Drain out the kidney beans and rinse them off. Place into pressure cooker and add in enough water to cover them up.
2. Place the lid on top and then turn on to a high pressure. When the steam starts to come out, lower it to medium and cook for about 30 minutes.
3. After this time, take the cooker from the stove and allow the pressure to lower on its own. Open the cooker and then add in the seasoning and vegetables. Mix it well.
4. Pour some water in the middle. Place the lid back on and cook for an additional 5 minutes.
5. When this is done, let the pressure go down and then enjoy.

Ratatouille

Ingredients:
3 Tbsp. olive oil
1 c. onion, chopped
1 ½ c. diced green bell peppers
2 sliced garlic cloves
1 ½ c. red bell peppers, diced
2 c. zucchini, diced
14 oz. diced tomatoes
2 c. eggplants, diced
¼ c. water
½ c. tomato sauce
½ tsp. thyme
¼ c. pepper
1 ½ tsp. salt
2 Tbsp. basil, shredded
2 Tbsp. balsamic vinegar
2 Tbsp. parsley

Directions:
1. Add in the peppers, garlic, and onions and brown them in the pressure cooker so that the onion can become soft.
2. Add in the pepper, salt, thyme, water, eggplant, tomatoes, and zucchini and brown these for another 4 minutes.
3. Cover the cooker and put it on a high pressure for about 5 minutes. Release pressure after this time and then remove the lid.
   Add in the parsley and basil and then adjust the seasonings to how you like them before serving. Enjoy!

Vegan Pasta Fagioli

Ingredients:

1 ½ c. beans, dried
2 Tbsp. olive oil
2 c. chopped onions
1 Tbsp. chopped garlic
2 chopped celery ribs
1 bay leaf
2 chopped carrots
1 ½ tsp. basil, dried
5 c. water, boiling
¼ tsp. red pepper flakes
3 Tbsp. tomato paste
1 c. shell pasta
1 tsp. salt
1 Tbsp. balsamic vinegar
¼ cup of nutritional yeast

Directions:

1. Take the beans and rinse and drain them off after they are done soaking. Set to the side.

2. In the pressure cooker, heat up the oil before adding the onion and letting it soften for 2 minutes.

3. Add the garlic in next and cook for 30 more seconds. Add in the boiling water, beans, spices, and the rest of the veggies. Lock the lid on the cooker and then bring it to a high pressure.

4. Reduce the heat a bit and cook the meal for about 5 minutes. When this is done you can allow the pressure to reduce a bit.

5. When you take the lid of, remove the bay leaf before stirring in the pasta and tomato paste. Cook for another 7 minutes to finish off the noodles.

6. Add in the vinegar last and top with some of the nutritional yeast before serving.

Double Dhal

Ingredients:
1 c. green lentil
1 ½ c. chana-dal
6 c. water, boiling
2 Tbsp. ginger, minced
10 minced garlic cloves
1 ½ tsp. of turmeric
8 chopped onions
3 tsp. cumin
2 tsp. garam masala
2 tsp. chili powder
Pepper
Salt
1 Tbsp. sultana
650 g. chopped potatoes
1 Tbsp. olive oil
500 g. chopped sweet potatoes

Directions:
1. Rinse off the lentils and the chana dal until the water begins to run clear. Heat up some oil in the pressure cooker and then add the garlic and onion and allow them to soften.
2. When this is done, add in the rest of the ingredients except the sultanas, salt, and garam masala.
3. Place the lid on top and bring to full pressure. When this is reached you can reduce the heat and cook it for 10 minutes.
4. After this time, release the pressure and slowly open the lid. Add in the remaining ingredients and add some more seasoning for taste.
5. If the meal is done, serve right away and enjoy!

Millet and Sweet Potatoes

Ingredients:

Stew

2 tsp. olive oil

1 ½ cups of millet

1 diced onion

½ tsp. cumin

¼ tsp. coriander

¼ tsp. turmeric

1 peeled and cubed sweet potato

2 tsp. harissa paste

2 c. vegetable broth

1 bag sliced spinach

Vinaigrette

2 Tbsp. sherry vinegar

2 Tbsp. lemon juice

1 tsp. olive oil

½ tsp. lemon zest, grated

1 tsp. maple syrup

Directions:

1. To start this stew, take out the pressure cooker and heat up the oil inside. Add the onions and let them cook for 2 minutes. Stir in the coriander, turmeric, cumin, and millet and cook for another 3 minutes before adding the harissa paste, broth, and sweet potato.
2. Close up the pressure cooker and bring it to a high pressure. Cook this meal for 9 minutes.
3. After it is done cooking, release the pressure. While that is cooling down you can work on the vinaigrette. To do this whisk lemon zest, maple syrup, oil, vinegar, and lemon juice.
4. Add this vinaigrette and the spinach in with the millet and stir. Season with some pepper and salt if you would like.

Curried Potatoes and Peas

Ingredients:
1 pkg. diced onions
2 tsp. melted butter
4 minced garlic cloves
1 ½ tsp. curry powder
2 tsp. ginger, minced
1 tsp. brown mustard seeds
6 Yukon gold potatoes
½ tsp. turmeric, ground
1 tsp. sugar
1 head cauliflower
1 c. thawed peas

Directions:

1. Heat up the butter inside the pressure cooker. When this is heated up, add the onions and let it cook for 3 minutes so they can soften. Add in the turmeric, mustard seeds, cumin, curry powder, ginger, and garlic and cook for another 2 minutes.
2. Add the sugar, cauliflower, potatoes, and half a cup of water. Close up the cooker and bring it to high pressure. Cook this for 5 minutes.
3. After this is done, release the pressure to cool down. Stir in the peas and then season with the pepper and salt. Serve this warm.

Provencal Vegetables

Ingredients:

2 garlic cloves
Pepper
Salt
2 Tbsp. olive oil
3 zucchini, sliced
4 tomatoes, crushed
3 eggplants, sliced
3 green peppers, sliced

Directions:

1. Take the eggplants and wash them before dicing and place into a dish rack. Sprinkle with some salt to get rid of the bitterness and allow them to set for about an hour before rinsing again.
2. Get the rest of the ingredients ready to go as well.
3. Heat up the oil inside a pressure cooker before adding in the garlic. Cook for a few minutes and add in ½ of tomatoes. Fry these for another 5 minutes at a high setting. Add in the rest of the vegetables and season.
4. Close the cooker and heat up to a high pressure. Reduce the heat a bit and cook for 4 minutes.
5. When this is done, allow the steam to leave. Place the vegetables into a dish and then serve right away.

Vegetable Porridge

Ingredients:

100 g. green beans
450 ml. vegetable broth
2 celery sticks
2 onions
Basil
1 carrot
1 zucchini
1 garlic clove
2 potatoes
100 g. peas

Directions:

1. Wash off all of the vegetables and get them prepared. Place the onion, garlic, and basil into a pressure cooker and mix to cook for 2 minutes.
2. Place the rest of the vegetables into the cooker and then cover with the broth. Turn the cooker onto a high pressure and let it cook for about 6 minutes.
3. When this is done, allow the steam to leave the pot and then season with the seasonings and basil. Serve warm and enjoy.

Miscellaneous Recipes

Lamb Shanks

Ingredients:

2 lbs. lamb shanks
Pepper
Salt
10 peeled garlic cloves
1 Tbsp. olive oil
½ c. port wine
½ c. chicken stock
1Tbsp.tomato paste
1 Tbsp. butter
½ tsp. rosemary, dried
1 tsp. balsamic vinegar

Directions:

1. Take the extra fat from the lamb shanks and then season with pepper and salt.
2. Heat up the oil in the cooker before adding the shanks into it as well and then brown all over.
3. Once the shanks are almost done you can add the garlic and then cook so that they can turn brown, but they do not burn.
4. Add the rosemary, tomato paste, port, and stock. Close the pressure cooker and then bring it up to a high pressure. Reduce the heat a bit to stabilize the pressure and then cook for about 30 minutes.

5. After this time, take the cooker from the heat and then allow the pressure to release. Take the shanks out before returning the cooker to a high heat.
6. Boil the liquid for about 5 minutes to get it to thicken into a sauce.
7. Whisk in the butter before adding the vinegar.
8. Serve this sauce on top of the lamb and enjoy.

Ham and Beans

Ingredients:

1 ½ lbs. ham
1 ½ lbs. white beans, dry
4½ c. water
1 minced garlic clove
1 diced yellow onion
1 bay leaf
Pepper
Salt

Directions:

1. Cut up the ham, garlic, and onion. Take the beans and rinse them off, making sure to get rid of any that are a little discolored.
2. Take out the pressure cooker and place all of the ingredients inside. Add some seasonings for taste.
3. Turn the cooker on to a high pressure. Cook the ingredients or about 25 minutes.
4. After the meal is cooked you should take out the bay leaf.

Serve with some cornbread or other side of your choice and enjoy.

Jambalaya

Ingredients:

8 oz. sliced sausage
½ Tbsp. oil
8 oz. chicken breast
8 oz. shrimp
½ tsp. thyme
1 tsp. Creole seasoning
1 dash cayenne pepper
1 chopped onion
1 chopped green bell pepper
3 minced garlic cloves
1 chopped jalapeno pepper
3 sliced celery stalks
1 tsp. Creole seasoning
1 dash hot sauce
2 c. canned tomatoes
1 c. white rice
3 Tbsp. minced parsley
1 c. chicken broth

Directions:

1. Take out the pressure cooker and turn it to the browning mode. Add in the shrimp, sausage, and chicken. Stir well.

2. Sprinkle the meats with the first amounts of cayenne, thyme, and seasoning. Cook it all together for 5 minutes, stirring often. Continue to cook until the meats are done. Use a slotted spoon and then set aside.

3. Add in the celery, peppers, garlic, and onion along with the rest of the seasonings. Cook this for 5 minutes and until the vegetables are done.

4. At this time add in the broth, tomatoes, and rice. Place the cover on top and bring it to a high pressure. Cook it for 8 minutes.

5. After this is done release the pressure and then add in the parsley along with the cooked meat. Cover and let stand for 5 minutes.

6. Serve warm.

Cornish Game Hens

Ingredients:

2 Tbsp. olive oil
1 Cornish hen
2 c. carrots
4 celery ribs
1 Tbsp. Worcestershire sauce
2 Tbsp. chopped garlic
2 tsp. Tabasco sauce
1/3 c. chopped green onion
2 Tbsp. chopped onion
Pepper
Salt
1 c. water

Directions:

1. Inside the pressure cooker and heat up the oil. Add in the Cornish hen and brown it for 3 minutes on all sides.
2. When this is done, combine the rest of ingredients in a bowl before pouring it on top of the hen.
3. Close the lid securely and then turn it on to a high pressure. Cook the meal at a high heat before turning the heat down a bit and cooking for another 15 minutes.
4. One this is done you should take the pressure of the heat and then allow the pressure to drop naturally.
5. Serve this warm with some vegetables or rice.

Sausage and German Potato Salad

Ingredients:

1 sliced onion
3 bacon slices
2 crushed garlic cloves
1/3 c. white wine vinegar
1/3 c. chicken broth
¾ tsp. salt
¼ tsp. dill weed
¼ tsp. white pepper
5 peeled and cubed potatoes
½ c. sour cream
1 lb. turkey sausage
½ tsp. dry mustard
1 minced green bell pepper
1/3 c. minced parsley
4 sliced radishes

Directions:

1. Take out the pressure cooker and sauté the bacon for 2 minutes so it becomes crisp. Add in the garlic and onion and cook for another 2 minutes.
2. Add in the dill, pepper, salt, vinegar, and broth and mix together well. Add in the sausage and potatoes.
3. Place the lid on to the cooker and turn it on to a high pressure. Reduce the heat a bit and let this cook for about 4 minutes. Release the pressure when done and then take the lid off.
4. Stir this mixture thoroughly and then add in the parsley, radishes, bell pepper, mustard, and sour cream. Toss to mix.
5. Pour this out into a bowl and then serve chilled or warm.

New England Dinner

Ingredients:

4 c. water
3 lbs. ham shank
12 halved potatoes
12 halved carrots
12 halved onions
1 cabbage
1 tsp. pepper

Directions:

1. Take out your pressure cooker and add in the water and the ham. Close it up with the lid. Turn the pressure on to a regular setting and cook the ham for 20 minutes.
2. When this is done, drop down the pressure and take the lid from the cooker. Add in the pepper and all of the vegetables.
3. Close the lid again and turn the pressure back up. Cook this meal for 8 minutes.
4. Serve warm.

Pork Enchiladas

Ingredients:
2 Tbsp. canola oil
1 lb. pork tenderloin
1 c. chicken broth
½ tsp. cumin
1 chopped onion
½ tsp. pepper
8 flour tortillas
1 ½ c. shredded cheddar cheese
1 c. sliced black olives
2 c. shredded Monterey jack cheese
1 c. chopped jalapeno pepper

Directions:
1. Take out the pressure cooker and heat up the oil. Add in the cumin, pork, pepper, and onions and cook so the pork can become browned.
2. Next, add in the chicken broth and cook for 15 minutes on a high pressure. When this is done, allow it to rest for a few minutes and then reduce the pressure.
3. Pour some of the sauce into a baking dish. Drain the pork of the broth and then place a little of this onto a tortilla.
4. Add some olives, cheese, and jalapenos as you would like and then roll the tortilla up and place into the baking dish. Do this for the rest of the tortillas.
5. Pour the rest of the sauce over the tortillas and top with cheese. Bake in the oven at a temperature of 350 degrees for 30 minutes.
6. When done, cool down for 10 minutes and then serve.

Curried Game Hens

Ingredients:

1 sliced onion
3 Cornish hens
1 crushed garlic clove
1 ½ c. chicken broth
1 tsp. Ginger
1 tsp. chili powder
1 Tbsp. curry powder
¼ c. cashews, chopped
3 Tbsp. yogurt

Directions:

1. Coat your pressure cooker with some cooking spray and then brown the garlic, onion, and hens together. Take the hens out of the cooker and tie their legs with a cheesecloth strip.
2. Place the hens back into the cooker and add the curry powder, ginger, chili powder, and broth. Bring this to a high pressure and then cook for about 8 minutes. Reduce the heat quickly.
3. Remove the hens and un-wrap them. Reduce the liquid a bit and then take from the heat. Add in the nuts and the yogurt to complete the sauce.
4. Place the hens on plates and top with the sauce to serve.

Gumbo

Ingredients:
3 chicken breasts
1 diced onion
2 kielbasa, sliced
3 diced carrots
1 c. pinto beans, dry
1 c. navy beans, dry
2 sweet corn ears
2 bouillon cubes, chicken
8 c. water
1 Tbsp. olive oil
3 Tbsp. garlic, chopped
Pepper
Salt
Spices

Directions:
1. Take the olive oil, water, corn cobs, carrots, onions, chicken, sausage, and beans and put them inside the pressure cooker.
2. Cover the cooker and let it get up to a full pressure. Cook this meal for 20 minutes. When this is done turn off the heat and let it cool down for 15 minutes.
3. Open up the cooker and remove the chicken and the cobs. Throw the cobs away and then tear up the chicken into smaller pieces. Place the chicken back into the cooker.
4. Add the rest of the ingredients to the cooker and bring them to boil. Add in a few seasonings before serving.

Tuscan Lamb

Ingredients:

3 ¼ c. of water
¾ c. northern beans
3 lbs. lamb shanks
2 Tbsp. flour, all purpose
½ tsp. salt
2 tsp. olive oil
½ tsp. pepper
½ c. sliced shallot
6 sliced garlic cloves
1 c. red wine, dry
1 tsp. rosemary
¼ c. sun dried tomatoes
1 Tbsp. Worcestershire sauce
2 Tbsp. chopped parsley
1 can beef broth
5 c. egg noodles

Directions:

1. Sort out and wash the beans and combine with 3 cups of water in a pan. Bring this to a boil and cook for a minute. Take off the heat and let soak for 20 minutes before draining and setting aside.
2. Trim the lamb before placing it into a bag with the pepper, salt, and flour. Shake in order to coat. Take the lamb out of the bag and shake the excess flour from it. Reserve some of the mixture and set it all to the side.
3. Bring out your pressure cooker and heat up some oil inside. Add one of the shanks and cook for 8 minutes so it becomes browned. Take it out of the pan and repeat with the rest of the lamb.

4. Add the garlic and shallots to the cooker and cook for 2 minutes. Add the ingredients through the both and then close the lid.
5. Turn the cooker to a high heat setting and cook for 7 minutes. Adjust the heat a bit and cook for another 45 minutes.
6. After this time, take the cooker off the heat and remove the lid. Take the lamb out and cool it completely.
7. Take the meat off the bones, and discard all but the meat.
8. Stir meat in with the bean mixture and sprinkle with parsley.
9. Serve this over noodles and enjoy.

Dessert Recipes

Chocolate Cake

Ingredients:
1½ c. flour, all purpose
3 Tbsp. cocoa powder
1 pinch salt
¾ Tbsp. baking powder
2 eggs
¼ c. melted butter
¾ c. sugar
2 Tsp. strawberry preserves
1 c. milk

Directions:
1. Take out a bowl and sift together the salt, baking powder, cocoa, and flour. In another bowl, beat the sugar and eggs so that the sugar can dissolve.
2. Add the preserves and melted butter to the eggs and mix well. Fold this egg mixture in with the flour mixture. Add in a little milk to get the batter to be thick and then beat so it becomes smooth.
3. Pour this batter into a greased pan. Put the pan into the pressure cooker and turn onto a high pressure with the lid on tight.
4. Steam for about 30 minutes. After this time you can take off the lid and let it steam for another 5 minutes.
5. Cool the cake down before taking out of pan and enjoying.

Mocha Cheesecake

Ingredients:

3 Tbsp. butter
¾ c. graham cracker crumbs, chocolate
¼ c. sugar
½ c. sugar
2 pkgs. Softened cream cheese
2 eggs
1 tsp. vanilla
¼ c. whipping cream
1 c. chocolate chips
3 Tbsp. coffee, brewed
3 Tbsp. Kahlua
Whipped cream

Directions:

1. Prepare your dish. Use a pan and line it with some foil.
2. Bring out a bowl and combine together the sugar, melted butter, cracker crumbs. Press this in the bottom of the pan and then set into the freezer until ready to use.
3. Take out another bowl and use an electric mixer to beat the sugar and cream cheese so they are smooth. Next, take the eggs and throw in one at a time. Beat in the eggs before adding the vanilla and whipping cream and beating some more.
4. Take out a pan and combine the Kahlua, chocolate chips, and coffee. Cook and then stir ingredients until melted.
5. Pour this hot mixture into the cheese and then beat the ingredients until combined. Spoon this into your prepared crust.
6. Bring your cooker out and place strips of foil into the bottom so that you can lower the cake into it. Pour 1 ½ cups of

water into the cooker and then set the trivet into the bottom so the cheesecake is not in the water.

7. Lock the lid of the cooker in place and then turn it up to a high pressure. Reduce the heat and then cook for about 15 minutes.

8. When the cake is done you can turn the heat off and let the pressure come out naturally. Take the lid off.

9. Lift the pan out of the cooker and then set it down to cool. Cover and place into the fridge to cool for a minimum of 4 hours before serving with some whipped cream and enjoy.

Pumpkin Bread Pudding

Ingredients:

5 slices cinnamon raisin bread, day old
2/3 c. canned pumpkin
2 Tbsp. butter
2 eggs
10 Tbsp. sugar
4 egg yolks
1 Tbsp. brandy
1 c. milk
1/8 tsp. salt
1 tsp. vanilla
Nutmeg
2 c. water

Directions:

1. Line a strainer using a paper towel. Add in the pumpkin and allow it to drain out for 30 minutes.
2. Take out a baking dish and butter it up. Spread out the slices of bread and butter one of the sides. Stack them up and then cut in small cubes.
3. In a bowl, whisk together the egg yolks, eggs, and sugar so they become light. Add the nutmeg, salt, vanilla, brandy, pumpkin, and milk and then mix it well. Pour this mixture all over the bread, making sure to press the bread down to absorb.
4. Place some foil into the baking pan before adding the bread. Add in a few cups of water to your pressure cooker before putting the baking pan into a steamer basket and then into the cooker.

5. Close the cooker and bring it to a high pressure. After this is reached reduce the heat a bit and cook for about 20 minutes.
6. When this is done, release the pressure and take the basket out. Pour any water that is on top of and then remove the foil.
7. Serve this warm and enjoy.

Rice Pudding

Ingredients:

2 c. sugar
1 c. uncooked white rice
Flavoring
5 c. milk

Directions:

1. Take out the pressure cooker and mix together all of the ingredients inside. Close the lid and turn on the cooker.
2. Let it come up to a high pressure until you get steam before placing weight on top.
3. Cook this dessert for about 25 minutes. When this is done, allow the cooker to cool down before you open it.
4. Serve this either hot or cold and enjoy.

Banana Pudding

Ingredients:
2 egg yolks
1 ripe banana
1 egg
3 Tbsp. sugar
¼ c. condensed milk, sweetened
½ c. half and half
¼ c. sour cream
½ tsp. vanilla
1 ½ tsp. of dark rum
2 c. water

Directions:
1. Take out four soufflé dishes to get started. In your food processor, puree the banana. Add in the vanilla, rum, sour cream, milk, and half and half and mix them all together well.
2. Strain out this mixture well with a fine strainer. Move to the soufflé dishes and then cover with some aluminum foil.
3. Place some water into the pressure cooker. Take a steamer basket and add in the dishes. Place this into the cooker and put the lid on top.
4. Allow the pressure to get high before reducing the heat a bit and cooking the mixture for 12 minutes.
5. When this is done, release the pressure right away and take the dishes out. Remove the foil.
6. Allow these to cool down. You can either eat them right away or store them for two days in the fridge to eat later.

Fruit and Honey

Ingredients:

¼ c. honey
2 c. water
½ lb. dried fruit, mixed
1 c. sliced carrot
½ c. raisins
¼ tsp. cinnamon
1 Tbsp. arrowroot
2 tsp. grated lemon rind
½ c. cashews

Directions:

1. Take out your pressure cooker and add in the honey and water. Allow this to come to a simmer. Add the lemon rind, cinnamon, carrots, raisins, and dried fruit next.
2. Close the lid and let it come to a high pressure. Then adjust the heat in order to stabilize the pressure and cook for about 5 minutes.
3. When this is done, take off the heat and release the pressure. Using a slotted spoon, remove the fruit.
4. Add in the arrowroot to the cooker and stir. Place the cashews and the liquid into a food processor to mix until they become smooth.
5. Serve the fruit inside a bowl and topped with the cashew cream. Enjoy!

Apple Crisp

Ingredients:

4 apples, peeled and sliced
½ c. oats, old fashioned
1 1/3 Tbsp. lemon juice
¼ c. flour
2 tsp. cinnamon
¼ c. brown sugar
4 Tbsp. butter
2/3 tsp. salt
1 c. water

Directions:

1. Take out a bowl and place the apples inside. Sprinkle with the lemon juice. Bring out another bowl and combine the butter, salt, cinnamon, brown sugar, flour, and oats.
2. Take the apples and place into a baking dish. Cover with the crisp mixture and then cover with foil.
3. Place this baking dish inside a pressure cooker and pour a cup of water into the pot as well.
4. Place the lid on top and lock it. Turn on to a high pressure and cook for 15 minutes. When it is done, allow the steam to release and remove the lid.
5. Take the apple crisp out of the cooker before removing the foil. Allow to cool for a few minutes before serving.

Crème Brulee

Ingredients:

¾ c. sugar
2 c. heavy cream
1 tsp. vanilla
1 c. warm water
4 egg yolks

Directions:

1. Mix all of the ingredients together besides the warm water. Fill up four ramekin dishes and then wrap with foil.
2. Place your inner pot inside the cooker and then pour a cup of water into the pot. Put the lid on top of the cooker and then lock the lid. Turn on the cooker and let it heat up to a high pressure.
3. Cook this for 4 minutes. When this is done, allow the steam to release and then take the lid off. Slowly take the ramekins out and then put into the fridge for a minimum of 3 hours to top.
4. When ready to serve, you can top with some sugar and caramelize the sugar in the broiler before eating.
5. Serve along with some fresh berries.

Chocolate Biscuits

Ingredients:

50 g white chocolate
180 g sugar
100 g melting chocolate
3 Tbsp. milk
180 g flour
1 Tbsp. cream
1 packet yeast
200 g butter
3 eggs

Directions:

1. Take out a Bundt pan and grease with some butter. In a pan you can place the white chocolate and add in some cream and milk. Heat it using the double boiler method, stirring to make a smooth cream.

2. Pour this into your pan, distributing it against the walls as good as you can.

3. Using the same method, melt the chocolate with the rest of the butter. Add in the milk and then mix to get a cream. Let it cool.

4. While that is heating up, beat the sugar and the eggs together for a few minutes before adding in the flour. Do this while alternating with the chocolate and melted butter.

5. Complete this with the yeast and then mix to get a good dough. Pour into the pan as well.

6. Pour some water into your pressure cooker and place the pan covered up inside. Close the cooker and allow it to reach a high pressure.

7. When this is done, reduce the heat and cook for 30 minutes. After this time, turn the heat off and allow the steam to escape a bit.

8. Let the pan cool a bit before taking out and then set for 10 more minutes before serving.

Caramel Flan

Ingredients:

1 stick vanilla
5 yolks
500 ml. milk
10 Tbsp. sugar

Directions:

1. Pick out the flan mold that you would like. Place it right on the heat of your pressure cooker. Add in a bit of water and 4 tablespoons of sugar and then make the caramel.
2. In a pan you can boil the milk for about 10 minutes along with the vanilla. When it is heated up, turn off the heat and allow it to cool.
3. Use a dipstick to beat the yolks together with the rest of the sugar and then mix so it becomes foamy. Add in the milk and mix to get a cream that is even. Place the cream into the mold.
4. Pour 300 ml. of water into the pressure cooker and place the mold inside. Close the lid and then cook for 30 minutes.
5. When it is done you can let the steam escape and take the mold out.
6. Cool in the fridge for about an hour before serving.

Conclusion

The pressure cooker is such a fantastically versatile appliance that can get dinner on the table in no time. As you can see from the recipes listed above, the meals are diverse, delicious, and take hardly any time at all to prepare. Now there is no excuse for why you cannot enjoy a delicious, nutritious meal even on the busiest of nights.

Reviews Request

Please help out a busy Mom and beginner author by leaving a review. It only takes a few minutes and means the world to me.

Jenny Jameson

Copyright Information Page

CPSIA information can be obtained
at www.ICGtesting.com
Printed in the USA
LVOW04s1052240916
506052LV00004B/32/P